The Journey of
THE WINTER ROSE
thoughts & rambles

by

Margery J. Kemp

Mountain House Press

Cover Design:
Margery J. Kemp
Katinka Kemp of
Katinka Kemp - services professionnels
(France)
& Guillaume Hingant of
Dragon Studio
(France)

Published 2019 by
Mountain House Press
526 Terania Creek Road
The Channon NSW 2480

ISBN 978-0-646-95274-1

Printed in Australia by
Ovato Book Printing
2019

for my family

By the same author

Poetry
THE TURN OF THE WHEEL
SHARDS OF GLASS
HEMISPHERES

Children's Poetry
I SPEAK YOU SPEAK

CONTENTS

Part One: **SPRING**

Part Four: **WINTER**

part one

SPRING

Deliverance

See that
White horse? It
Has no rider.

Thorns though
Remain on the
Sand; quite

Dangerous in
Fact, so that
The horse

Treads judiciously
Around them
With a

Delicacy
That speaks of
Satisfaction,

As the rider
Catches a
Wave; steps

From sharp
Sea; knots her
Hair seductively

Above
Her neck and
Walks towards

The man
Who walks
Towards her.

Embryo

The stage is set,
The curtain swings

Times good
Or bad

Wait in the wings.

The Expert

Yoga is compatible
With Mozart, and so
It seems is the ear
Of the whip bird-
Transfixed outside
The bedroom door, its

Mate soon attracted
Also as part of the
Act: the Ave Verum
Corpus interspersed
By an equally familiar
Legato-staccato duet
Of pitch and clarity
Unmatched by honed
Leather's mimicking
Crack. With

Clipped turns on
Rhythmic sticks of
Pencil lead, one
Small, dark, feathery
Figure hops through
The door, cocks its
Crest and surveys
My strange, stretched
Salute before fanning
Its tail in disbelief,
As if to say –

"That's not the way
To learn to fly."

Once in a London Garden
(according to Shakespeare)

Roses were red,
Roses were white;

Pink was the stream
Which carried the night

Into deep waters
Of Tudor delight.

Swallows

1. Arrival – the Nest above the Window

Seasonal differential
Is announced

Not by climatic
Altercation

But by the return
Of the first

Swallow.

2. Departure

You've flown. The
Verandah silence

Is startling without
The threatening swish

Of your wings about
Us or above our

Heads (familiar as we
Once shared a house

With micro bats). Now
We hope for your chicks

Safe passage from
Home above the

Rafters to far away
Places & from

Innocence to wisdom –
See you next year?

A Moment of Peace can be ....

A tiny spark
In a dark place

Or a deep breath
In the cosmic turbulence.

Night Thoughts

Slowly the mind concedes
The end of the day.

Complexity rests,
Yet rises, with

The articulation of
Itself no longer lost.

Technology Balance

When technology inhibits
The senses

It should no longer
Be permitted

To inhabit the soul.

The Anniversary

The room is bright, brittle
With years sustained, not by
Solace, but by discriminating
Company. The hosts have been
Married for sixty
Years. The company
Is upstanding
For the toast.

Speeches evoke
The distinguished
Courtship. Faded sepia
Bears witness to
Seemly convention. The
Celebration hums with
Conservative gentility.

Generations ripple
The overview. Enter

The flowing feral: the
Dreadlocked grandchild.

Displacement

1. Do We Really want to Move

Accompanied
By the agent
Our nomadic spirits
Take us house

Hunting: from
Point A to point
B; never in a
Straight line.

From pink walls &
Lace curtains,
Beneath low
Ceilings through

Dark passages
Yawning onto
Steep land,
Overlooking

Close neighbours
In strong
Winds along
Rough roads

Back onto
Highways circum-
Navigating our
Restlessness;

Finally
Laying ghosts
Beyond our own
Front door.

2. Moving House

With these words
I exist in space – not

My space but
Moving space

Between two places, one
Replete, & one

Slowly filling
With silence.

3. A Gipsy Heart

I try to imagine
What it's like to arrive

But I only know
What it's like to travel

Long journeys of the mind
& the body resigned

To resting places
Never called home.

My spiritual home
Was one of these

& in my heart
I put its seed

To germinate
& wait for the homecoming.

Symbols of Imperfection

Home, house,
Garden;

Frenetic, untidy,
Abundant;

Candles, incense,
Music;

Verandah, birdsong,
Stretches:

*

Holistic.

Small Thoughts

The science of dreams
Is analysis;

The science of science
Is dreams.

*

Synthesis
Is yesterday

Before it becomes
Tomorrow.

Cat

1. Cat caress

Hand
Caresses cat;

Cat caresses
Mind; cat

……….. As muse – is
That why

I called you Sappho?

2. Cat Space

With eyes on the prize
Cat leaps on my chair;
Stretches & grooms
'Till I too sit there.

Two green pools blaze,
There is no room to spare.
Cat moves, sits on knee,
Deems compromise fair!

3. Benediction

The cat

The sun salute

Vivaldi

A perfect minute.

Diverse Reality

The tangency of reality
Can be equally invoked

By a cosmic treatise

Or a recipe for bread.

Reflections

The mirror
Is dusty; the
Woman is
Comforted
By the absence
Of sharp detail
In line and
Lustre.

The child
Stands by the lake,
Relishing the sun
Drenched image
Of her bright
Countenance
In the rising mist.

Macro Moments

1.
Today on the dark street
Winter stole from spring

A moment of clarity.

2.
A sense of grail
From other days returns

But fleetingly abides

No longer than this minute
In the mind.

3.
Tonight, a small
Chink of light finds
Its way into my

Heart: a
Ratchet in
The tower wall.

The Cross

1.
The cross is
Mighty, raises

Hate &
Being great,

In this
World & the

Next seals
Lucifer's fate.

2.
A jewel
Is at the centre of
The cross,
Which burns
In every corner
Of the earth;

& eyes
Can't quench the flames
Of freedom passed

Into its
Blazing heart.

Morning Abstraction

Dictated by the vagaries
Of breakfast radio,
Beethoven follows

Hildergarde: chastening
The honed passion of her
Canticles; negating

A need for the
Choral whisper, the
Treble note rising,

The spire which
Inspires, the vocal
Heights which heal.

A Changing Constant

The mind rises
Beyond shopping bags

Groceries & footsteps
On pavements

Which mark the
Time governed

By age &
Circumstances

& liberated by
Discipline of self.

A Taste of Peace

What is she trying
To achieve, alone in the
Church, its portals neither
Binding her thoughts nor

Reaching the nearest
Ley line? And who am I
To judge, who struggles daily
With the influx

Of souls unwanted
In my life; who can't
Shift ghosts, it seems
Not yet! That day

Will come, I know, but,
In the meantime
I must resign myself
To the grinding wheel

Of events beyond
My control, while angry
Men resist the narrow
Road to their hearts,

And others ache. Lady
In the church, maybe
I should join you. At least
You wait in comfort.

Rock on

They've rocked around the cosmic clock,
One with love & one with mind.

They'll rock until they have to stop:
Says love to wisdom, "be my guide".

Part two

SUMMER

The Storm

On Christmas
Day the cemetery
Bends with the
Black clouds which
Follow us as we
Drive up the
Hill. We

Leave flowers, the
Skies open and
We don't linger
For what has now
Become a gentle
Mellowing of
Reflection on the
Present, rather than
A harrowing disgorging
Of the past. Five
Days later we
Return to acknowledge
A birthday, this
Time a little
Downcast without
Flowers from a storm-
Denuded garden to
Discover

The storm's
Gift. Dancing
Across the grass
Carpets of pale
Pink orchids give
Joy to the day.

To Love or Lose

A passport shrinks
Distance, but

For two
People in different

Hemispheres, love
Will not

Shrink distance
Without sacrifice.

Vision

1.
In the eye of the storm
There are no directions:

We are in the middle
Of nothing

& the middle of
Everything.

2.
There is an awakening
Of things
That have come
To be:

There was a time to mourn;

Now it's a time
To see.

3.
The enemy departs
In many stages,

Each stage
Widening the horizon

Until, with the
Final departure,

We are the horizon.

Cyclonic Destruction

The tail still
Thrashes – all

That remains
Of the anger

Attempts to lash
The land in futility

In the wake
Of the circuitous

Crescendo of pain.

Seasonal Spectrum

Biting the apple
Of winter we walk
Through the forest
Of our dreams,
Knowing that the
Shifting sands
Will be unresolved
By the lunar
Metronome. Sleet

Nails our morning
Thoughts – we
Read them, shred
Them in the

Spring, and burn

Them in the summer.

Koalas

He beckons them
Through the door then
Places his finger
On his lips in
A salute to silence.
The mid-day temperature
Soars to thirty

Five degrees as they
File in behind him, stand
Like soldiers in
The herbs and lift
Their eyes into the
Branches of the bleeding
Heart tree. Four

Eyes meet theirs and
Four furry ears
Listen. Two soft, grey
Forms shift as four
Sets of small,
Sharp, dark claws
Release and firmly
Re-position – oh
HAPPY BEAR DAY, shouts
The youngest

Of the human
Tribe, and the larger
Koala moves to acknowledge
Parentage to the accompaniment

Of a choral SHUSH!

Bridges

1.
Yesterday's strength

Is today's sadness &

Tomorrow's power.

2.
Where does unconditional love end &
Self preservation begin?

Night Fisherman

Breeze tempers
Flame; ice

Melts as
Waves no more

Are cold
Contrast to

Caustic haze: the
Fisherman's

Feet sink
Into the sand's

Hypnotic ways;
Embraces

He his
Mistress,

Sensuous beach;
The soporific

Evening her
Caress; the

Blanket
Of the night

This sage
Placates.

Nurture

Fingers in earth
A meal, notes

In a journal –
Dessert.

*

Plants feed
The soul,

Weeds
Feed the

Mind &
The harvest

Feeds the body.

Pond Life

Frogs spiel
A steady
Stream of sound;

Birds break water into ripples
On the wing, soaring
Swiftly to safety;

Dragon flies hover & hum
Over rampant weeds, depart
Laterally like aliens;

Goldfish mouthe
Aphasic warnings to
The dog, who

From a distance bounds
& slides indelicately
Into the water, rising

As a mutable, green
Monster, from the last
Lonely waterlily.

Nice

There is a limit to
                    nice

Nice music, nice
Incense

Nice meditation,

    & oh, nice peace,

    But –

Jo's fit last night ....

& the need for observation

    in the morning.

Yesterday Revisited

1.

From the mountain
To the valley, this
Place like another
Where dreams were

Spent, again seduces
With its chimera. I
Stop my routine &
Let every muscle

Speak; the domino
Effect of repressed
Tension is once
More acknowledged.

2.

In the form
Of shame or

Pride, memory
Is governed

By ego.

Karmic Correction

A life
Torn from strife;

A voice,
Shouting till noise

Was mind.
Only thought could bind

Soul
& body as whole;

Silent screaming
Redeeming

Incarnation.
Communication

Prevailing,
Assailing;

The unsolicited
Terminated;

The afternoon
Still bitter-sweet.

Call from Katinka

You ring me to say
The clock has stopped –

No, not your alarm
Clock, but the Martin

Place clock: the clock
Of our mythology: the old

Sydney GPO tower clock,
Under which familial tales

Of romantic liaisons
Are legendary, &, I add,

On the steps below which
A street photographer

Captured the essence of
A war with a melting image

Of a uniformed airman
& his elegant wife: a

Photograph of your
Grandparents which has

Pride of place in your
Life. Let me know,

Won't you,
When the clock starts.

The Way it is

The radio, the

Purr of the cat,

The circumference

Of birds, the frogs

Delight in dampness,

Footsteps down

The hall, a hen's

Declaration of

Its egg: the

Essence of being.

Morning Coffee

At the table next
To mine three
Generations are
Seated – the

Child, kneeling on
Her plastic sandals,
Is served milk froth
In the smallest cup
With the smallest
Saucer on which
Is placed the
Smallest spoon which
Soon adorns the smallest
Nose with the whitest
Foam, while

The mother from
The tallest cup slowly
Sips a latte and with
A napkin wipes the
Smallest nose almost
But not quite, clean,

As the grandmother
With the roundest
Cup and cappuccino
Evidence in mind,
Retrieves a tissue from
A vinyl shopping bag,
For herself and for
The smallest one, who
With it pats the oldest
Lips and then the
Smallest nose, ensuring,
For them both, faces

For the street.

Market Trio

He wears tattoos
& juggles balls
With hair in spikes
& one rat's tail.

His bare brown feet
& harem pants
& ankle beads
Define his dance.

He raps; she sings
A low lament,
A Celtic hymn
With slow amens

For all the pain
Of hope defiled
By Erin's saints.
The thin violin

Defines a new
Tune of praise.
This trinity
Their voices raise.

The Desert Rose

Blood still stains the
Rose, its petals

Red with summer.

    *

Wisdom
Is tired
Of trying to proclaim herself,

Love
Loses the battle
To lust,

& shadows
Are defended
With guns.

From David – a fragile Farewell

In this dream

He stands on the edge
Of a deep ravine

At the helm of
An astral army

& raises his arm in salute
To us in the distance

As a testament
To our resolution.

The Artist

He dips his brush
In the color
Of today

And harnesses yesterday
As a gift
For tomorrow.

Part three

Autumn

Birds and Glass Houses

An arid sound terminates
The flight path
With a shock that

Decimates the senses.
A dropped plate vies
For attention; succeeds,

As we engage in damage
Control, gathering
Shards before

Stepping in reparation
Through glass doors and
Carefully lifting

The bright fruit
Pigeon; tenderly caressing
An emerald wing and

Thankfully restoring
Undamaged wholeness
Once more to height.

A State of balance

To read
To write
To think

Is this life
Of soul.

The rest

Is prudence & care
For those in need.

*

 A confidential journey
Above & below

Transported
By mind

Unseen but
Precipitous

Assesses eternity.

*

The need to escape
Is intellectual

When the mind's stagnation,
Bursting out

Of the repetition of tasks
Master-minded by time,

Challenges
Holistic wellness.

Greatness

1.
In being glorious
There may be no glory,

But in finding
Glory, there will be peace.

2.
Physical fools are often
Spiritual giants.

Aspects of a journey

Years close doors; friendships
Linger, cling, then fade,

Ending the search for
Self – the greatest friend.

*

Age robs time: to clean,
To cook, to consume

Satisfies body
But not mind

Until
Time robs age;

Grants mind
Vision.

Audrey

With a jolt I
Read of your death: the

Gallery is for sale
& the coin man misses

His old friend .... We trod
Our London path

Last year in ignorance
& recollection

& now our daughter
Has travelled from Paris

To Bloomsbury in memory
Of joy & sadness. She

Texts that she is walking
Through the square

Towards your old home,
Invoking love & remorse

As your presence
Looms large.

The Matriarch

Never more divisive
Than after her death
Their mother
Kindles her ashes
And boils them
A cauldron
Of her sacrifice.

One daughter
Grabs with heavy hands
The spoils, one
Feigns at
Reticence and one

Stands back and sighs.
It is the immutable
Pound of flesh
Of her silence

That they divide.

Bequests

1.
The picture in the frame

Is the goodness imprisoned
When the heart has flown

And the soul keeps secrets.

2.
Perhaps the written word

Is merely a cryptic expression

Of a snapshot

Of the molecule of meaning.

Python

1. The Carpet Snake's way Home

Lizzie-in-the-roof
Not that way,
Through the daisies
& along the verandah
Floor where Josephine
Is sitting. Heed

The vociferous
Dog & know that
Mutual respect will
Win the day, &
Necessitate a
Change in your

Rite of passage
Leading to the
Rafters & the door-
Way to your home: the
Gap twixt wall
& roof – providing

of course, you have
not over-eaten!

2. Adversaries

You'd hardly call them friends
Lizzie-in-the-roof
& Martha.

Not enemies either,
But fellow vigilantes.

Tormentor & tormented,

Rat exterminator
& people deterer,

The one – silent & sensuous;
The other garrulous & guileless.

Carpet snake & black dog,

Power brokers in territories
Determined by the
Ancient cat.

Josephine, Autism & Self Esteem

We've waited long time
For this occasion –
Both social &
Functional. Always

Your hair has been cut
By me, mum ...... on the
Run ...... a random experience
Of changing style; scissors

In one hand, comb in the
Other, your mood questionable,
In the light of this intrusion
On time & personal space.

Now, Sue is here,
With basket, salon scissors,
Comb, towel & mirror,
Perception & skill.

Seated on the verandah your
Movements are disaffected,
Then glad, as you look
From one of us, to the other.

Hair falls in thick
Layers; the dog sniffs
& fusses as it drifts
in a breeze towards

her food ......

                    it's over
& the mirror tells all –
That you're beautiful

& you know it!

Metamorphic

The aim of atonement

Is mental self sufficiency

Unencumbered by the seeking

Of those who would praise or gratify.

Writing ....

1.
Writing
Is a lifeline in darkness.

2.
To write each day
Is a good thing

From the point of view
Of skill maintenance
& thought relevance

& even
To feed martyrdom.

3.
I moderate

Meandering
Thoughts to

Punctuate the day.

It Happens

The daughter
Is twenty five

& the mother
At sixty is

No longer
Invincible

But a thread-
Bare deity

Destined to
Be immortalized

In a painted
Shroud.

His Last Town March – an Anzac Day Farewell

He sat this year
    Upon a seat
Collapsible
    Beside the road,
A garden seat
    Brought to the site
Beside him, in
    His daughter's car,
From which had spilled
    Along the way,
Grandchildren heed-
    Lessly absorbed,
Each to each one's
    Own pursuit on
This incongruous
    Holiday.

She kissed her
    Father; did
Not stay with him on
    This auspicious
Day for those who
    Waited by the
Road, beneath thin
    Early morning
Sun, which beat,
    By noon, late
April's way, full
    On the swelling
Hearts of those
    Who watched, and warmed

The road for those
        Whose frail feet
With old diggers
        Marched .... Beyond

The dream
        The battle
Man, marched to
        The tune of
Jungle guns and
        Mortars, shells
And absent friends
        In combat
Lost, or culled
        With age.

Security Check

At the regional airport I pass
Through security

Before boarding the flight to
Sydney.

A female security officer indicates her
Need for

Further checking. I step to the
Side as indicated.

The officer proceeds with verbal
Formalities. No I

Have no problems with this
Routine. I then open

My handbag as requested. A cursory
Glance at the

Contents is followed by a discussion
Of my handbag – the

Design, the colour & the quality
Of the leather: the brand

& place of purchase: the security
Officer would like

A bag like mine. We assess regional
Shopping.

The security check is over. I prepare
To board my plane.

Mmm ....

1.
Resurrect
Yesterday's faults &

Put them on the map

Without shame.

2.
I have
Spent my life

Making mistakes

& not being much the wiser!

Druid

She stood
In the centre of
The storm: in the eye,

& in that moment
Knew transition, &
Everything changed.

Cycles & journeys
Prevailed until all was
Whole & contained,

& her world was
governed by circles
& rays, & sex

Was the magician's tool.

Nimbin

1.
This quintessential
Energy of stone sits
On a verdant throne;

A womb for many, for
Some a tomb,

For others just a home.

2.
A sword in the
Stone raises
Fire, sets sparks

In the mist as
Dreams, which
Destroy or inspire.

3.
A twitch upon the thread.

Song City

The youngest sibling.
When she was two (her sister said)
Commenced to sing,

& everywhere she went,
She sang a song about roses
Which was popular at the time,

To such an extent
That her small voice
Was soon well known,

& people commented
On pitch & clarity
& purity of tone.

*

As a result, her mother
Taught her more
Songs, mainly Scottish,

Like "Annie Laurie"
& "The Road to the Isles",
& her toneless father,

When he returned from
The war, taught her drinking
Songs to sing out of tune.

*

Her older sister regretted
Teaching her pop songs, for she hid
Behind the sofa & sang lyrics

About engagement rings in the presence
Of her sister's shy boyfriend,
Causing embarrassment.

                *

She sang each night in bed,
& while waiting for sleep
Placed each song in a song city,

Which never changed
But grew in comfort
& familiarity.

                *

A river ran through her city,
Wide & busy,
With a bridge,

& each song
Allocated itself a place
& the song city spread –

"The owl and the Pussycat", for
Example, was some distance
From the river, & several

Nursery rhymes even reached
The country, where lanes were
Narrow & gardens bright.

*

But she always returned
To the wide & busy
River, & the familiarity

Of the city, which was the
Home of the song
About roses.

*

She married & taught
Her daughters the songs
Of the song city,

& finally travelled
To London
With her husband,

Where her
Mind gained
Momentum

*

As lanes,
Roads,
Bridges,
Palaces,
Chimes & churches...........

Yielded her songs.

The Song

My signature
Is a song.

*

This song
Is a love song

For a man
& a woman

& a family
As it was
As it is &
As it shall be.

For friendship now,

& friends that return
In memory & dreams.

*

First the poem,
Then the song.

Annihilation Paris 2015

Silent souls

Shout in
In bloodied ether

An anachronism
Of sound

Crying for alignment.

*

From a distance
This crisis
Stills our minds

The road ahead
Mutates, the
Seasons roll

& on our backs
We carry the past

Transcended.

Home

1.
To return home
Is to return to infinity

2.
Build me a new home
With the poetry of the old,

Leaving behind
The laboured prose.

3.
To the lost house of dreams
I dreamed

I returned to your whiteness
This time seen.

Part four

WINTER

Something Saved

The day is soft
& wet & full
Of inconvenience
But returns us
To the womb of
Your childhood. The
Heart still holds
A small spark of
Fear to be quenched
By melded tears;
& this place,
So alien, to which
I came, is filled
With the spirit
Of a new beginning.

The next small step
Will see the start
Of karmic gain.

Four Irish Moments

1.
Let me have
An Irish blessing

Not expressed
In words already

Written – there are
Many of those,

But in spoken
Words & greetings,

& images of
Mists & hills,

Winding roads &
Secreted lakes,

Towns & villages
Beyond which the sea

Opens in broad vistas
To the world.

2.
This sanctuary
Is an enigma &

Men so salacious
& affable, affectionate

& benignly censorious
Of their women,

Profoundly &
Curiously

Relinquish
Their hearts

To its stern
Caress.

3.
Surely the essence
Of Ireland is a mother

Who has waited
& watched &

Tolerated her children
With a jaundiced

Eye knowing that
One day they would

Understand that she
Has no favourites.

4.
Should I abandon
The archaeological
Diggings of the

Psyche & lighten
The load? This
I have considered,

But I have returned
From Ireland with
The sun on my

Back: a sun as
Warm as the waters
Of the womb.

I write again.

Acceptance

When life has ceased to move
In one direction

Reaction to its style is often shame

Till time earns gain.

*

To be the bane
Of the ignorant

Is an honour
& a trial.

*

On the road to the end
There is nothing to prove.

Silence & Search

Meditation is the search
For the universe
As self .... Silence

Is the imperceptible rapidity
Of the vibration
Of eternity.

Love Lost

They dance
In an inspired forest

Of knots
& tangles,

Vicissitudes
Falling

From heaven's
Canopy

Between heaven
& hell.

Unfinished Business

A fleeting glance
Invokes the easy
Yesterdays, unchallenged
By the karmic
Arbiter. Why

Should we seek to
Meet again, to
Scratch contemplatively
The soul; to wound

The psyche of the
Mind not quite
At peace with its ideals?

Let us not yet face
The metamorphosis.
We will know the price
We pay with the next

Encounter, when only the
Soul will be familiar.

An Aspect of Family

1. Felicity & Josephine

Two wise women
Are seated beside me,
Faces glowing
With delayed
Incandescence
Etched with knives
Melting
In amber furnaces.

Autism passes
Like shadows:
Voices
Find tomorrow,
Enunciating sacrifice.

*2. With Felicity – Testing the Contents
of a Dusty Box*

Vinyl rediscovered
Turns your thoughts

To lyrics which
Stretched the soul

As the resonant
Voices rise
To bite the mind.

3. Autistic Speak

She struggles, speaks
A word, then

A sentence – I get it,
We laugh! It's

The comfort
Of expression,

That calms the crying heart.

4. Karma

I am content
To let others

Hold my life
In their hands;

This is specific
As are their needs.

   *
It has been this way
For endless years

Of strength
& weakness

Resolve &
Vacillation,

Termination
& renewal

Precision
& precipice.

*

Restoration prevails
Through the eye of a needle,

& for the duration
The road will be straight.

5. Aspirations

Self-first
In the light
Of the needs of others
Entails routine
Exercise
Harmony
Music
An environment to please
A garden
Love of others & therefore

Sacrifice of self.

News Report

"Information teleported from
Light to matter." Suddenly

Ancient wisdom becomes
An item in the daily news.

The mystic's armour of
Stealth is disregarded; the

Scorn & shame
Likewise. The magician's

Persecution for the occult
Practices of ages past,

& the heretic's burning
Become superfluous,

Displaced by the narcissism
Of the necessity for truth.

For Helen

This plane
Is late
By three hours,

Delayed
By fog:

The fog
Which carries
Me
North

To the
Funeral,

Like a sacred
Shroud.

＊

Still,
I shall arrive
On time,

Descending
From the
Clouds

In a salute

To your
Departing;

Carrying,
In my

Handbag,

Your eulogy.

Genealogy

The breath of life
Descends

Through castles
& gutters; ascends

Backwards;

De-synthesises.

The Winter Rose

Conceding nothing
But the beauty
Of her stride
To the lingering glances
Of the passers-by
She is bereft of
Souls familiar
With her cause,
Now the effect
Of burning
In the desert
Of her worth.

She saw, she spoke, she
Died the heretic's death
Upon the metaphorical
Stake, her petals ash beyond
The flames – the mystic
Rose, the daughter
Of the god within
Her soul, her shame,
Her sin,

Returns; wakes
In blanched
Light, white petals
On white ice. The
Ether diffuses, and
The heart that
Swells, lost
Hope foretells.

A Wish

I would like to be back
On a track stepping down
To a creek

With a small waterfall
Once more to sit beside,

To hear the rise
Of the notes that
Poetry sings

& to catch the words
as they spill.

On being a Rock

Sometimes
I would like

To languish,
Let myself go

Along the path
Of aging decadence

Most people take

Without consideration –

Without
Care required

In the absence of need.

But ....

Wellbeing
Matters

When needs,
Governed by love,

Want

Cornerstones.

Small Karma

The perpetrator who broods
On elemental matters
Relating to a victim

May cause the psyche of the
Victim to ache
With self protection

Until the perpetrator's self
Is hopefully stilled
With a dart's return.

Intermezzo

This soul
Is hidden;

This peace
Is busy;

This solitude
Festers, seeks

Music, please.

Voice trails piano keys –
Oh, my sweet

High C, how
I've missed you!

Poetry

May poetry be always

A song
Of the soul.

*

Poetry............

A macrocosm
Of thought in

A microcosm
Of word.

*

Poetry is a pilgrimage.

The Gipsy Song

The road winds back to beaches,
Mountains and a gipsy singing on
A path, reading his palm while he
Crossed hers with silver, citing
The song. At the base of a volcanic
Neck was solitude; at the shore
Was the birth of idealism,
Transcended then, on rolling hills,
To a song.

It was the song that filled
The air with waves that
Finally shattered the soul
Expanding the ether with the
Shock of pain.

The words gained momentum,
With the immediacy of contrition
And declaration, minus
Absolution. The sore

Heart, though, continued to
Dance in the eyes of
Others whose lives were still
Driven by idealism as they
Pondered at length on the external
Nature of things other than
Themselves. He knew them too well,
And feared for their frailty in the
Hands of self knowledge, which

Came finally with the thawing
Of the tears of winter sweetening
the bitter ground, yielding
the roses which were there
at the beginning of the road,

Even before the song.

Genetically Speaking

Results ....
Endings:

*

Blameless,
Shameless;

*

 Silence
The soul.

Sisters

For Katinka – June, 2015

This small affirmation of your recent time with Felicity comes again with love and thanks: life or death – which? Finally, for Fe, life, & thanks go to a speedy & efficient emergency team at Lismore Base, a top surgical team at the Gold Coast, & you.

You were there when the decision was made to transfer Fe from Lismore to the Gold Coast for emergency surgery, & without hesitation you climbed into the ambulance & remained with her for the next five days in only the clothes you were wearing (hole in jeans testament to this!). With her care & communication needs, & a mattress provided for you on the floor of ICU, you reputedly made the difference, & I quote the surgeon who later stated of you - "she's one in a million".

Sisters.

From Katinka – June, 2016

"One year on from one of the most heartbreaking of days, of weeks... we nearly lost you, you stayed. And though sometimes the weight of the world bears down a little too much, there's not a thing I'd change... a life shared, full of richness and meaning.

Sisters."

The Wheel

Time is new,
& you are born
On a brooding
Sultry morn,

Where starts a path
Beyond my heart;
Beyond the
Heart that's played its part.

The stones are rough,
The branches sting
& as I watch
I softly sing,

Knowing that your limbs
Are strong,
Your mind is firmly
Set, & wrong

Can touch you
But not set you back,
As your first steps
On life's long track

Are taken hand in
Hand with he,
Who opens gates,
& sets you free.

To Verity & Kirsten

Pilgrims of the soul
Beyond our tethered hearts,

Your ether challenges,
& your arms stretch Heaven

As we heed
The gift of love.

Moon Tide

To those

Who've found joy

On a long road

I salute you.

About the author

Born in Orange New South Wales and raised in Sydney, Margery Kemp lives with retired Radiologist husband Tim in The Channon area of the New South Wales Northern Rivers hinterland. They have raised a complex family of beautiful daughters, and the family story is woven into the writings of her poetry.

A Children's Hospital trained nurse, her focus over the years has been holistic health research and family care. She believes in music as therapy, has a passion for singing, and was a pupil of the late Welsh tenor David Parker.

Though known as Jill which is her middle name, she writes as Margery Kemp in tribute to her fifteenth century namesake Margery Kempe of Lynn, who was the first woman to write an autobiography in English.

The Journey of THE WINTER ROSE thoughts & rambles, is her fifth collection.